Unveiled

A Poetry Memoir

IVY CIRILLO

Unveiled: A Poetry Memoir
Copyright © 2019 by Ivy Cirillo

First paperback edition August 2019

Book Design by Ivy Cirillo
Cover Illustration by Zed Baldemor
Additional Illustration by Paz Cravero

ISBN 978-1-7332356-0-0 (Paperback)
ISBN 978-1-7332356-1-7 (eBook)

Published by Orion Publishing House
www.orionpublishinghouse.com

ATTENTION: SCHOOLS AND BUSIESSES
Orion Publishing House books are available at quantity discounts with bulk purchase for educational, business, or sales promotional use. For information, please e-mail Orion Publishing House: info@orionpublishinghouse.com

Dedicated to the —
Souls that need healing,
Voices that need hearing,
& Hearts that need mending.

Inside me,
there has always been a story
itching to come out.

Scratching at the surface,
and demanding to be told.

Until now,
I've suppressed it.

Feeling the need
to keep it hidden,
and keep it mine.

But now,
it's time
for the unveiling.

Each of us has a story,
and this one is mine.

MY
STORY

MY EARLIEST MEMORY

My earliest memory
will stay with me forever.

The blood,
The tears,
The screams,
& The tiring effort of the rescue team.

This is where my story began.

A MOTHER'S LOVE

I will never forget
the day you told me
that I'm like a bug
that just won't die.

MOTHER DAUGHTER RELATIONSHIPS

A child
should not have to beg
their mother for a relationship.

Nor should they have to watch
their mother give that relationship
to someone else.

WASTED TIME

I wish I had known then
that I was wasting my time.

I shouldn't have had to beg
for a relationship with you.

I shouldn't have had to hope
that I would get one
after your sister's death.

But worse of all,
I shouldn't have to watch
you treat someone else
better than your own daughter.

A FATHER'S GIFT

My scars,
My name,
& All of my tears.

You've gifted these things to me.

You gave me life
and almost death.

You made me who I am.

A lover,
a fighter.

Stronger than you,
smarter than you.

Thank you for these gifts.

BECAUSE OF YOU

I shed these tears,
because of you.

I have these scars,
because of you.

I have this name,
because of you.

I have these fears,
because of you.

I am stronger,
because of you.

I will forever be me,
because of you.

A LOST CHILD

When you die,
I will not
mourn the loss of you.

Instead, I will
mourn the loss of the relationship
that I never got to have with you.

SHITTY ART

My mom likes to tell this story
of how I once took off my diaper
& used its contents to paint the walls
of her bedroom closet,

But what she doesn't share
is that said closet
was my so called nursery.

Even in diapers
I knew that was wrong,
and I stood up for myself.

GROWING UP

When others were enjoying their childhood,
I was doing anything but.

Instead of focusing on school,
I was wondering if I could trust my mother.

Instead of being scared of spiders,
I was terrified of my father.

Instead of enjoying life,
I was raising my brother.

I was told I wasn't the parent of the household,
but someone had to be.

A GRAIN OF SALT.

Growing up,
I was fed endless lies
about my father.

I grew up terrified
of what he was
and what he did.

I spent way too much time
hating him and wondering
why I wasn't good enough.

Only to realize,
that I didn't have
both sides of the story.

I FORGIVE YOU

At the age of sixteen,
I forgave the man that tried to kill me.

I gathered up all of the newspaper clippings,
I found all of the police reports,
I read the testimonies,
& I made a decision.

As crazy as it sounds,
he thought he was doing
what was best for me.

And looking back,
I commend him for that.

So I began the path to forgiveness.

I prayed about it,
I forgave him in my heart,
& I wrote him a letter,
but I never found the courage to send it.

So if you're reading this,
just know that I forgive you.

CAN YOU FORGIVE ME?

I may have forgiven you,
but that doesn't erase all of my fears.

I still feel the need to —

Watch my back,
Avoid unknown callers,
Double check my surroundings,
Fight off nightmares,
& Keep my location private.

It's not so much that I'm afraid of you,
I'm just afraid of what might happen,
what could happen.

I'm just not ready to meet you yet.
Please forgive me.

Raised in a Bar

I didn't realize it then,
but I was born into
a family of alcoholics.

Every day after work,
we'd head over
to City Limits.

At first,
I thought it was
the perfect set up.

Under the TV,
the bartenders kept
a special box of toys.

They'd feed us chicken tenders
and let us use the claw machine,
which I quickly learned to empty out.

Everyone knew me by name,
even if I didn't have the slightest clue
as to who they were.

Though that didn't matter,
because I knew that
I'd see them tomorrow.

CHILDHOOD ANXIETIES

A little girl
should never
have to worry if —

Her mother is cheating on her husband,
Her father will escape from prison,
Her home will be raided for drugs,
Or her parents will end up dead.

But I guess,
I was never a little girl,
just a young lady
trapped in a child's body.

YOUR LEGACY

How it must've hurt
to realize that
your daughter would
be greater than you.

Maybe that's why
you told me
to drop out of school
12 days before graduation.

WHERE THE BLAME FALLS

I don't think you ever realized
just how selfish you could be.

You blamed me for the life you didn't have
and you voiced it quite often.

You drank and did so stupidly
without ever considering the consequences.

You denied the hospital when you clearly needed stitches
leaving me to watch you sleep and make sure you didn't die.

You happily interfered with my life
with no disregard for my plans.

But you were all too eager
to let me know when my life disrupted yours.

Which I guess,
was all the damn time.

A DIFFERENT KIND OF MARRIAGE

So many children
long for their parents
to get back together,
but I was different.

Instead, I desperately wanted
for them to get a divorce.

Their fighting was toxic
and I couldn't take it anymore.

The only time they got along
was long enough for sex,
and then it was back to fighting again.

Now and then,
my dad would pack up his stuff and drive off
only for my mom to call him and tell him to come back.

And on occasion,
it would be my mom who packed us up
and said we were staying at her sister's house.

I quickly grew tired of this
and then I grew up.

HOME LIFE

I told you it was toxic
and you laughed in my face.

Thank you for proving my point.

RUNAWAY

I tried to run away once,
but had nowhere to go.

So I sat under a tree
and read a book
until you forced me home.

MUDFEST

We fell asleep,
with her older brother's friend
in between us.

We didn't think
anything of it
at the time.

But later that night,
I felt something on my face.

I pretended to be asleep
and rolled over,
using the blanket
to carefully wipe it off.

I heard laughing,
feet skittering,
and car doors
slamming shut.

The next day,
I found out
that my friend
had been raped.

And years later,
I realized,
I'd been assaulted too.

DEAR OLD FRIENDS

To all the friends
I've loved
and lost,
just know
that I forgive you.

I understand
our time
was limited.

But please know,
that your secrets,
will forever
remain sealed.

& You can always
find a friend
in me.

HOMES AWAY FROM HOME

To my best friends' parents,
I want to say thank you.

Thank you
for giving me
the love and respect
that I didn't find at home.

Thank you
for giving me
a safe place to hide
when life became too dark.

But most of all,
thank you
for giving me
the very children
that are my best friends.

GENETICS

"You look just like her"
they used to say.

But deep down, they didn't know
how wholeheartedly
I tried to be anything but.

BREAKING THE CYCLE

Often times I'm asked,
"how did you end up like this?"

And more often than not,
I want to reply,
"I don't know"
but I'd be lying.

Truthfully,
it wasn't by accident.

It took every ounce of me
not to follow in my family's footsteps.

I looked at my parents
and used them as an example of how not to act.

They drank,
so I didn't.

They smoked,
so I didn't.

They did drugs,
so I didn't.

They got pregnant,
so I didn't.

And it wasn't just what they did do,
it was what they didn't do as well.

They didn't finish high school,
so I did.

They didn't go to college,
so I did.

They didn't have a plan,
so I did.

I made sure to do and be
the very opposite of them.

That's how I ended up this way.

THE TRUTH HURTS

If I told you
why my parents kicked me out
you'd think that I was lying.

But when I tell you,
it was over a TV remote,
it's the God's honest truth.

Of course,
I've got a few theories of my own —

Like the fact that
I didn't agree with their life choices.

Or that I no longer gave them
the money to fuel their addictions.

Either way though,
I'm glad that I was able
to get out of that house.

Even if,
it was a little earlier
than I had originally planned.

WHAT CONSTITUTES A PERFECT CHILD?

I was the child
that got straight A's
but skipped school to get my parents' attention.

I was the child
that got in trouble for reading during lectures
because it was the only place that I could escape to.

I was the child
that excelled in everything I did
but constantly wondered if I was good enough.

To everyone else,
I was the perfect child,
but not to those that birthed me.

SIBLINGS

No matter how hard
I tried to be
the perfect child,
I always got it wrong.

And for some reason,
my brother and I
had different expectations.

My parents expected
the world from me,
but treated him
as if he were the world.

To them,
he could do no wrong,
and I was envious of that.

Nevertheless,
I was still happy
to take the crap
that he would have been dealt.

I did my best
to shield him
from my parent's wrath.

And after I left,
I always wondered,
if they took it out on him too.

Silent Therapy

When you struggle with mental illness,
it's suggested that you see a therapist.

But what they don't tell you
is that it's not a safe space.

You still have to censor your words
and make sure to avoid any hot topics.

So even though,
I was considering suicide,
I knew I couldn't talk about it.

And even though,
I was afraid for my brother,
I couldn't talk about that either.

So it wasn't long
before I made the decision
to just stop talking altogether.

PARENTHOOD

As far as I'm concerned,
you are not a parent if —

You constantly think
that your child is faking their pain.

You blame them
for the unhappiness in your life.

You borrow money from them
to support your bad habits.

Or you force them
to fend for themselves.

I could continue,
but I digress.

MY MOTHER'S PAST

Many years ago,
I came to the conclusion
that the pain of my mother's past
had shaped her into the woman that stood before me.

That is the reason she never grew up,
That is the reason she never matured,
& That is the reason she never became the mother that I
needed her to be.

For that, I do not blame her.
But what I do blame her for
is not putting in more of an effort
towards putting her past behind her.

DEPENDENCE

Was it too much of me to ask you —

Not to stagger around drunk in public,
Not to get high when my friends were over,
& Not to have sex while making us dinner?

Was it too much for me to be born?

Or was it just too much for me to depend on you?

THE NICE ONES ALWAYS FINISH LAST

I'll never understand
how you could choose
everything else
over me.

It didn't matter if it was —

Your sister,
Your friends,
Your alcohol,
Or your drugs.

No matter what,
I always felt
like I was last in line.

THE NEW YOU

After all this time,
I can see that you're changing
and I appreciate the effort.

But if I'm being honest,
I just can't find it in myself
to wish you a "Happy Mother's Day."

Especially,
when all you've ever done
is act like anything but.

UNSPOKEN PAIN

You can't imagine
the pang of guilt I feel,
each time you tell me
you love me.

But I just can't find it in my heart
to say "I love you" back.

It's been a long time
since I've learned
to live without you,
and it's not easy
accepting you back
into my life again.

THE CURSE OF BLOOD

Loyalty
is a funny thing.

You can treat me like shit,
Take my money,
& Leave me homeless.

But for some reason,
I still feel the need
to defend you.

THE GIVING ME

The Giving Tree
was my favorite book
when I was a kid.

I guess that explains
why I'm constantly giving,
without getting
anything in return.

Unpopularity

Being unpopular
isn't just about
not having friends.

It's inviting people you hate
to your birthday party,
because all of your "friends"
laughed at your invitation.

THE RUMOR MILL

Rumors spread
like wildfire,
one that I couldn't contain.

I was a gorilla
because of my hair.

I was a vampire
because of my skin.

And I was emo
because of my scars.

These words seem so trivial now,
but there was a time
when they almost broke me.

I'M SORRY

I became a bully,
because I was bullied.

And for that,
I'll always be remorseful.

ACCEPTED

Ever since I can remember
I have wanted to go to college.

I joined clubs in elementary school
and truly began to focus on my grades.

Not because I wanted to get in,
but because I had to.

College wasn't just about the degree,
it was about getting out of the house.

I knew that if I could secure enough funds
I would finally be free.

Free from the toxins,
Free from the lies,
& Free from my family.

So I did all that I could do
until I finally received that big envelope,
and the six more that followed.

REGRETS

They're few and far between,
but that doesn't mean
that I don't still have them.

I just keep them hidden
from the public, and try my best
to forget them myself.

Nevertheless, I regret —

Not saving myself,
Never getting baptized,
& A few other things that
I'd rather not discuss.

FAMILIAL TIES

What some parents don't realize
is that everything they say and do
is being watched and mentally noted.

It is because of this
that I have such a distorted view
on both marriage and motherhood.

From my perspective,
they both consisted of yelling,
unhappiness,
and hurt.

It is the reason,
that I constantly questioned
whether or not I could be
a good mother or a good wife.

Still to this day,
I am unsure
of my capabilities.

BROKEN SMILES

For years,
I constantly hid my pain
and learned to fake a smile.

That way, no one would know
what went on at home.

That way, no one would know
just how much I hurt.

& That way, no one would know
just how bad things really were.

THANKS DOC

A doctor once told me,
"you're too young
for more than one illness;
and that's why no doctor
will take you seriously."

Since that day,
I've over gone tests,
surgeries, and treatments,
& my medical chart now reads:

Hypothyroidism
Hashimoto's Thyroiditis
PTSD
Astigmatism
Anxiety
Depression
Lupus
CREST
Fibromyalgia
IBS
Chronic Sinusitis
Chronic Tonsillitis
Eye Toxicity
Restrictive Lung Disease
Lung Nodules
Pulmonary Hypertension
Fatty Liver
Dysautonomia
Chronic Migraines
Sleep Apnea
& More

Had I lacked the strength
to argue with you
and advocate for myself
who knows where I'd be today.

FAMILY TREE

When I really think about it,
we don't have anyone left.

Aunts,
Uncles,
& Grandparents;
Everyone before us has died.

It's just me,
My mom,
& My brother.

And I can only assume,
that I'm next.

THE C WORD

To me,
there's nothing scarier than the C word.

All of my life,
I've used it as a comparison.

I have Lupus,
but at least it's not cancer.

I have Hypothyroidism,
but at least it's not cancer.

I have Dysautonomia,
but at least it's not cancer.

I have Fibromyalgia,
but at least it's not cancer.

So you can surely imagine,
how terrified I was,
when I thought I had lung cancer.

And unfortunately,
it's still too early
to rule anything out.

A WILL TO LIVE

With multiple surgeries
and countless procedures
under my belt.

I've never once been prepared
when the nurses ask
for my living will.

The Truth About Being Okay

"But you're going to be okay right?"

This is a question I'm asked often,
but I don't always know how to respond.

So instead, I lie.
But here's the truth —

If okay is
taking medications every day
for an illness without a cure,

If okay is
constantly wondering
how much longer you can go on,

If okay is
accepting the simple truth
that you will probably die young,

Then I guess,
according to you,
I'll be okay.

EXPECTATIONS

For the longest time,
I tried so hard to be
who everyone else
wanted me to be.

The honors student.
The perfect daughter.
The best friend.

And somewhere
along the way,
I managed to lose myself.

The Unveiling

To conceal my past
would be admittance
that I am ashamed of it.

To conceal my past
would give others the impression
that what they did was acceptable.

To conceal my past
would prevent me from not only
sharing my story, but growing from it.

Therefore,
I will not conceal my past;
consider it unveiled.

MY STORY

My story may be sad,
but it doesn't mean
that I have to be.

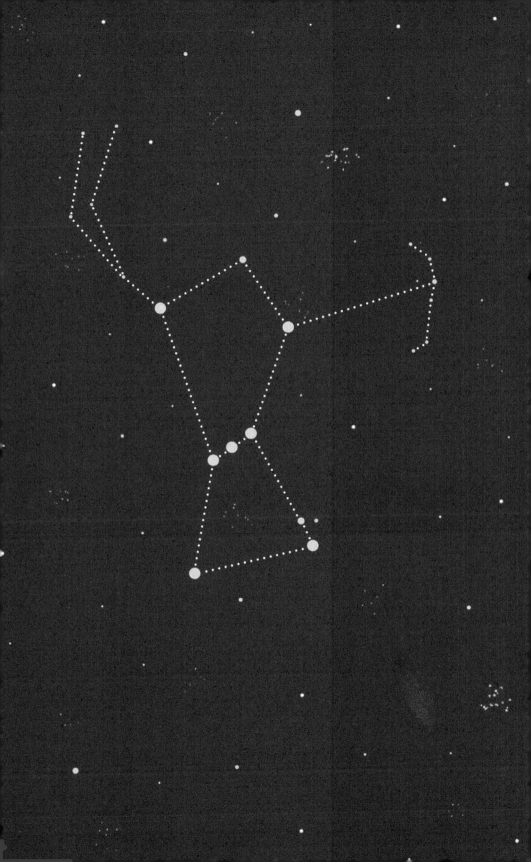

MY

PAIN

PAIN IS POETRY

It's moments like this
when the words come easily.

The emotions flow through me
dripping right onto the page.

MEAN GIRL

I am not
the kind of person
to sugarcoat my words.

In me
you'll find honesty
even if it stings.

MIXED EMOTIONS

There are days
when I'm full of emotion
tightly sealed like a bottle.

Then there are days
when I can't feel a thing
and I'm completely void inside.

MY DEAR FRIEND

Loss
is not a simple concept.
Especially when it's tragic.

And not
a single day goes by,
that I don't still think of you.

APPARITIONS

Sometimes,
I feel like a ghost.

Someone
that was once here,
but has since been forgotten.

A distant memory,
and nothing more.

INDEPENDENT

What once was,
is now lost.

And all I'm left with
is me, myself, and I.

WARY

Oh, how I used to wish
that you would finally change.

That you'd realize your wrongdoings
and apologize for all the pain.

But now that you're doing so
I'm not sure what to do.

How can I be positive,
that the words you say are true?

TRUST ISSUES

Trust,
is just a way to let your guard down.

A way to show you care,
just enough to be broken.

A way to fall,
then find out no one is there to catch you.

A way to know who will stick around,
when no one else does.

A way to show,
just how naive you really are.

Tell me,
is it worth it?

DETACHED

Emotionless
I lay still
in a bed
of my own pity.

Heartbroken.

THE ANGEL OF DEATH

I often think of death
and it doesn't seem to scare me.

Maybe that's
what I should be afraid of.

SILENT PRAYERS

Someday I wish,
to have the strength
to move forward.

To rid myself of —

My thoughts
My doubts
My anxieties
& My depression.

But for now,
I pray.

Strength or Lack Thereof

On days like today,
I am grateful
that I am not stronger.

For I do not have
the strength
to end my suffering.

FAILED ASSUMPTIONS

Silent judgement
can sometimes be
worse than hateful words.

I often wish that
people would inquire,
rather than coming
to their own conclusions.

Give me a chance
to explain myself.

The story isn't always
what you assume it to be.

SACRED SCARS

It does not matter
if the scars
are physical
or emotional.

They are there.
They are permanent.
They are yours.

Embrace them.

HOLDING ON

The pain
I feel inside
is getting harder
and harder
to hide.

A single thing,
so small,
can put me on the edge.

It takes everything
that I am
and will be
to keep myself
from jumping.

THE DEVIL WITHIN

There are demons
inside each of us
begging to be heard.

Unknowingly,
slipping out
little by little –

In our actions,
In our thoughts,
& In our words.

We must keep them at bay,
recognizing their existence,
but not giving in to them.

GREAT EXPECTATIONS

Sometimes,
more often than not,
I expect too much
and quite frequently
it leads to disappointment.

Yet sometimes,
I disappoint myself,
because I feel like
I should be able to
expect these things from others.

HIDE AND SEEK

My pulse can be
difficult to find
and I often wonder
the reason behind it.

Is it because
I'm stuck all alone
on a plane of my own existence?

Or maybe because
I'm caught in between
the shadows of life and death?

Or maybe it's because
even my pulse knows
that I don't want to be here,
so it hides too.

A WORLD OF PAIN

Without sight
I can't see the world;

But I can still feel
the pain it's caused me.

Without sound,
I can't hear the world;

But I still know
someone is crying.

BITTERSWEET RELIEF

It's in these moments
of pure exhaustion
when I finally feel at peace.

My body is prepared for rest
and my head has finally slowed;
for once, there's no —

      Stressful thoughts,
      Hidden anxieties,
      Or hateful comments.

My mind is blank
and free of them all,
at least for the time being.

MAN VS. SELF

The hate you give,
burns deep inside.

But I promise,
I can withstand the flames.

You can't possibly hate me,
more than I already hate myself.

GUARDED

I have great reason
to keep my walls up.

To guard myself
from the aches and pains
that others can bring me.

To protect myself
from getting hurt.

While unintentionally,
shielding myself
from the possibility of love.

THINGS I'LL NEVER GET USED TO

No matter how much
I try to keep up
with everyone else,
there's just some things
that I'll never get used to.

Like —

Knowing that I'm sick
and there isn't a cure.

Coming to the realization
that I may never finish my degree.

Or that I may never have the strength
to bear or raise a child.

TRANSFERENCE

The human heart
knows no bounds.

Yes, there are two ventricles
but there are also;

A never-ending stream of emotions
that will forever flow through them.

MISFIT

In a world
full of beautiful people,

I constantly feel
like an outsider.

ADMIRATION

I have always loved —

80s movies,
YA books,
Polaroid cameras,
& Old typewriters.

But never myself.

UNFORTHCOMING

My biggest mistake
is devoting so much of my life
to people that don't share theirs with me.

EMPTY WORDS

Apologies don't mean a thing.

They're nothing more
than a string of words
in any given order.

Frankly, it is the actions
following an apology
that speak the truth.

So, keep your
"I'm sorry's" to yourself
and think before you act.

LOSING CONSCIOUSNESS

I am broken,
shattered like glass.

And no matter how hard I try
to pick myself up
and put myself back together again,
I just can't do it.

My hands are bleeding
and I am sinking
further and further
into this ocean of despair.

THE DISAPPOINTING TRUTH

I've never been able
to accept a compliment.

Not because I'm asking for them,
or fishing for more.

But simply because,
I've never seen the truth in them.

REFLECTIONS

I struggle with my image
and the added pounds that I've acquired.

You tell me I look healthier,
but I just don't see it.

Instead, I see —

Clothes far larger than I used to wear,
A round face and a double chin,
& Extra curves where I used to be thin.

I hate the way my arms look huge
and the way my legs are bulky;
but mostly, I just hate the fact
that my body has done this to me.

I didn't get a say in my weight
and I can't change it
no matter the measures I take.

Pills, diets, and the like
have zero chance
of winning this fight.

For now, I guess
I'll just wear a body
that isn't mine.

MUSINGS

I used to think
that I was fat
when I was a size 0.

So you can only imagine
just how disgusted
I am with myself
as a size 18.

SELF-INFLICTED PAIN

Each afternoon,
a bumble bee
buzzes around my yard.

Before throwing itself
repeatedly
at the glass window
on the far wall.

What a pity
it must be
to purposely
inflict
that kind of pain
onto one's self.

When will it learn?

ENDLESS POSSIBILITIES

I am often distracted
by simple moments
that did not occur.

The could have,
would have,
should have beens.

Oh how they haunt me.

UNSEWN TAPESTRIES

There's a hole in me;
a missing piece,
an unfillable void.

I now recognize though,
that it wasn't a flaw
in my design.

Instead,
it was an opening
and it has a purpose.

How else
would the pain,
the hurt,
& the darkness
seep in?

It was bound to break through eventually.

MISSING PIECES

Sometimes I feel
unfinished —

As if God has forgotten
an integral piece
that should have gone
into making me.

Is that piece out there somewhere?
Is that why I struggle to find myself?

Because there is still a part of me
waiting to be pushed inside
the puzzle — that is me?

HOPELESS OPTIMISTIC

Pain washes over me
when I think about the things
that I let slip through my fingertips.

Missed opportunities,
wishing for a second chance
the kind that will never present itself.

CONSUMED

Like melted chocolate
on fingertips.

I've been devoured
and not a drop of me is left.

CAN YOU PLEASE?

Can you please
help me see
this person
that I'm meant to be?

Can you help me
through this pain
and give me hope
for another day?

Can you be here
thick and through
to help me achieve
all that I can do?

I didn't think so.

THE SUFFERING OF OTHERS

According to you
it could be worse.

But you'll never know
what I struggle with.

The aches and pains
of chronic illness.

The anxieties and doubts
of mental illness.

Who are you
to decide if my pain is worthy?

Who are you
to decide if my suffering qualifies?

This isn't easy,
and as far as I can see,
it can't get much worse.

TELL ME.

How do you overcome the pain
when you feel restricted
and caged,
but worse.

Like a butterfly
caught in the intricate web
of an all too eager spider.

Struggling for your life
but knowing that the end is near
and no matter how hard you try
you're drawn to it.

MISGUIDED BRAVERY

Bravery —
the act of showing great courage.

I've been labeled brave,
but sadly, you've been misinformed.

I'm simply just trying to survive.

MY PAIN

How often I wish
that I could forget
the pain that I've endured.

The cuts I bore,
The tears I cried,
& The time I wasted.

HAPPINESS IS A LUXURY

If happiness
were easy to find,
we wouldn't snatch it
so greedily from others.

SECLUDED

Even in
the presence
of others,
I still feel alone.

HAUNTING MEMORIES

Memories
follow me around
like a ghost,
haunting me
just like
my other demons.

MELANCHOLY

Sadness drapes over me
like a scarf in chilly weather.

But I don't wear it
like a fashion statement.

Instead, it wears me.

NIGHT TERRORS

When darkness meets the light
and day turns into night,

That's when my fears roam free
sending me to purgatory.

SELF-HATE DEFINED

Self-hate is
avoiding each one of your reflections
whether you're passing yourself in
a mirror,
a window,
or a glass surface.

Self-hate is
doing a double take
just to silently judge
yourself,
your reflection,
& your body.

SCATTERED BEINGS

My thoughts are scattered
inside my head,

Like the glow-in-the-dark stars
above your bed.

Each one there
with its own purpose,

Driving me crazy
like an amateur circus.

DISAPPEARING ACT

Loneliness
is an emotion
that I feel
wholeheartedly.

Forever alone
in a crowded space
full of people
invisible to the eye.

THE OUTFIELD

There's something bittersweet about —

Watching your friends graduate,
when you wish it could be you.

Congratulating friends on pregnancies,
like the ones you'll never have.

And seeing happiness shared between friends,
when you feel completely alone.

Chronic illness
has all but taken my life,
so now I'm forced to sit and watch
everyone else's from the sidelines.

DISTANCE

My heart aches
in the form of jealousy.

For the friends
that no longer be
& for the friends
I can no longer see.

I miss them,
but do they miss me?

BUSY BODY

If I took a moment
to stop and write
all of the thoughts
that pop into my head,

I would spend
days upon days
with a pen in my hand
never finishing
all the things
that needed to be said.

NATURAL DISASTER

If the weather
mimicked my emotions
it would constantly be changing.

There'd be torrential downpours,
and flash floods,
and droughts.

The world would be
in a constant state
of unpredictability.

As if it weren't already.

HIDDEN

Sometimes
I wish
the darker clouds
would overcome
my body.

Swallow me whole
and stash me away
where no one
would be able
to find me.

MOURNING

Each day that I wake
I've managed to escape
Death's tight embrace.

But I don't always wish that I did.

PLEASANTRIES

I appreciate conversation,
but not when it is forced.

So don't ask me how I am,
if you don't really care.

And don't ask me if I'll get better,
if you can't handle the truth.

I promise not to get upset, as long as
you don't waste anymore of my time.

MIRRORS

Others may look at you
and think
that they know you.

But only you
can see
your true reflection.

Only you
know the pain and torment
that you've experienced.

& Only you
can understand
the struggles that you've faced.

INTERNAL CONFLICT

When your body
is constantly battling itself
you often look for reassurance.

In doctors,
In test results,
In loved ones,
& In yourself.

You can't help
but hope and pray
that things will get better.

Often wishing
you had a bit of pixie dust
to help make things a little easier.

LIFELINE

I've been cursed
to feel too intensely —

Rage burns like fire
beneath my skin

& My tears threaten
to drown me.

Please tell me,
how do I save myself?

BETTER DAYS

Occasionally,
I dream of the day
when I won't wake up again.

Or at the very least,
I'll wake up
but my pain
will have disappeared.

Almost as if,
I had been cleansed of it
and washed anew.

Oh, how I wish
that day would come soon.

BULLET PROOF

More often than not,
my heart is shot

With anxiety
depression
and grief.

I mourn the loss of my past life
and the future that will never be.

I long for the greatness
the kind that I should have been.

The greatness I could have been
had I not been overcome with illness.

Some days are harder than others
and some day are worse.

I just can't let it get the best of me.

THE LIGHT AT THE END OF THE TUNNEL

A deep depression
has overcome me.
Though I am not scared.

Eventually,
I will move past this.

Past the pain.
Past the hate.
Past the thoughts of self-harm.

I am stronger than this
and I will prevail.
I have to.

FORGIVENESS

Forgive and forget
that's what they always say,
but how do you forgive —

The father that tried to kill you,
The mother that was too selfish to care,
The stepfather that kicked you out,
The brother that doesn't return your calls,
The grandparents that left you too early, or
The friends that gave up on you?

You just do,
because you have to do what's right for you.

You have to forgive others,
so you can take care of yourself.

A lesson I learned the hard way.

LETTING GO

Can we take a moment
to talk about my pain
and acknowledge that it exists?

Now, can we take a moment
to move forward
and free ourselves from this?

RESTORATION

Stubbornness does not change the fact
that sometimes, we must surrender.

We must forgive ourselves
for the pain that we've caused
and begin the journey of healing.

WHAT IF

Sometimes I wonder
what could have been —

Had my father murdered me.
Had my brother died.
Had I gotten to know my unborn sibling.
Had I been adopted.
Had I killed myself.

But then I realize,
I would not be
who I am
without these life events.

The pain of my story
is what made me.

THE BIGGER PICTURE

Not everything
will fall into place
just as we wish it to be.

The events of our lives
are meant to piece together
a bigger picture; and we must let them
even if we do not understand it ourselves.

SHATTERED STRENGTH

Inside me,
you will find —

A broken heart
and shattered glass.

And alongside that,
you will find —

The strength
to move mountains.

NOT FOR PROFIT

With these words
I will bring you immortality
and for a split second
I will question my thinking.

Then, I'll realize
that the importance
of sharing my story
far outweighs
the thought of you
benefiting from it.

CHRONIC PAIN

My illnesses —
they are a blessing in disguise,
and sometimes I forget that.

But, I'm thankful for the pain,
because it reminds me that I can feel
and that I'm strong enough to survive this.

AN ODE TO YOU

Through the tears and sorrow
I find solace in knowing
that I am not alone.

There's You
& Me
& God.

DARKNESS TO LIGHT

I have found inspiration
in my darkest moments,

And in those moments
I've found the writer in me.

Those are the moments
that I wouldn't wish on anyone,

And yet, I'm thankful for them
because they've brought me to you.

My wonderfully supportive readers.

MY
FUTURE

DISTRACTED

And for a moment there
I almost forgot

That I have the strength
and the power
to pursue my passions.

And I won't ever let that happen again.

MY FUTURE

Is it selfish to hope
for a future greater than yours?

No.

It's human for you
to want what's best
for yourself.

You deserve it,
& don't ever let yourself forget that.

BEAUTY

Beauty is in everything
no matter where you look.

So keep your eyes peeled
and soak it in.

Find inspiration in the ordinary.

DISCOVERING BEAUTY

Beauty is love,
love from the heart.
A heart filled with joy,
right from the start.

Find your beauty.

CRYSTAL DREAMS

In my dreams
I hope to see
the person that
I'm meant to be.

Only our subconscious knows
our greatest desires;
and the passions which will burn
the brightest fires.

So come to me
my sweet dreams
and show me who
I'm meant to be.

STICKS & STONES

The world will throw advice at you
most of which is unwanted
but every once in awhile
you will stumble upon
a pebble of wisdom.

NEW BEGINNINGS

If the day can end
and begin anew,
don't you deserve
to start over too?

STRUGGLING PROFUSELY

Long before I knew my life's purpose,
I struggled —

To find myself,
To fit in,
To be invisible,
& To be me.

My only hope is that in the future,
my struggles will not have been for nothing.

Revelations

I don't remember the day
when my dreams began to change
but I wish I had listened to my heart
from the beginning.

Whether I dreamt of being —

A ballerina,
A teacher,
A writer,
Or the like;

I never should have
let my dreams change
based on my fears
of being without money.

AN AUTHOR'S INNER THOUGHTS

As I write this,
I wonder —

Will readers flock
to the words I write
like I do the works
of the authors I admire,

Or will they put them
on their bookshelves
and save them
for a rainy day?

A JOURNEY WITH WORDS

I never thought
I would be a writer,

But looking back
it should have been clear.

In my darkest hours
I clung to my notebook.

& In my happiest moments
poetry flowed from my fingertips.

Whether I realized it or not,
I was born a writer

And I look forward to pursuing this passion
for years to come.

ECSTASY

Like a crystal
bathing in the moonlight,
I dream of being cleansed.

Cleansed of my impurities,
Cleansed of my insecurities,
& Cleansed of my inhibitions.

For I deserve happiness.
Pure, unfiltered, happiness.
And so do you.

SELF-LOVE

There are still times
when I look in the mirror
and I can't help but notice my flaws.

Self-love isn't instantaneous
and I'd never expect it to be,
but with continuous practice
I'll learn to love myself completely.

DEAR FUTURE SELF

Dear future self,
don't ever
fall so far from grace
into a place
full of so much
hate and self-doubt
that you can't
come back
from it.

Dear future self,
don't ever
get to the point
when you are
so damaged
that you can't possibly
accept what you
truly deserve.

Dear future self,
do everything
in your power
to find your
happy place
and stay there
for as long
as your soul
can take.

LEARNING TO LOVE MYSELF

Years from now
I hope to see,
a better version
of myself
looking back
at me.

Smile lines,
angel kisses,
and all.

HEAVEN

There are days
when the only thing
that can keep me going
is the awe & wonder of the day
when I will enter the Kingdom of God.

That is my future.

MY TRIBE

One day, I hope to find
the place where I belong
and the people that I belong with.

RECKLESS

Is to shape one's future
on someone else,

When there are no guarantees
and no promises.

So take your time,
find your passions,
and pursue them.

If it's the only thing you do
you will have done it right.

THE ART OF HEALING

To heal is to grow
& I hope to do both
in the near future.

FUTURE PEACE

In the future,
I hope to be in a place
where I no longer feel guilty
for taking a moment to care for myself.

PERSEVERANCE

Life is difficult
but if you
find your path
& surround yourself
with loved ones
the hard times
won't be so trying.

JUST BE YOU

It's ok to be fragile
and it's ok to be strong.

Just be unapologetically
and unequivocally you.

SURVIVAL OF THE FITTEST

There will be times
when you have to learn
when to pick your battles.

And there will be times
when you have to fight so fiercely
that you almost forget
what it is you're fighting for.

RELENTLESS

It's hard to find strength
in the pain
that you've endured,
but you have to,
for this I am sure.

Now,
I won't tell you
that it will be easy,
but I know for a fact
that it will be worth it.

CONSTANT COMPARISONS

Each one of us
compares ourselves
to someone else.

But how different
the world would be
if we only compared ourselves
to alternate versions
of ourselves.

We could grow from our past selves
and learn from our future selves.

We could focus on our achievements
instead of our failures.

& We could seek improvement
instead of judging others.

Can you imagine
the kind of world
we could be living in?

SOCIAL CHANGE

Perhaps, the world will change
and society will see
that it's okay to be —

Unique,
Accepting,
& Independent.

God knows I am.
And I long for the day
when others are too.

BLOSSOMING BEAUTIES

Cherry blossoms
sweet and serene.

True beauty
begging to be seen.

You should see yourself
this way too.

Because you are true beauty
when you're just being you.

IMPENETRABLE BLISS

I want a life full of impenetrable bliss.

I want to find my passion
and pursue it with all my might.

I want to travel the world
and tackle every mountain in sight.

I want to love unconditionally
and hold onto it so very tight.

I want the life I've dreamed of,
a life full of love and light.

NO TRUER CLICHES

No matter the pain you've gone through
or the pain that you may endure,
you must be —

The flower
that breaks through the concrete.

The rainbow
that emerges from the storm.

& The diamond
that hides in the rough.

UNAPOLOGETICALLY ME

I won't apologize
for the way that I am.

It's taken years to shape and mold me.
And even longer to learn to love me.
But I am, unapologetically me.

I have tiger stripes
and big brown eyes.

I have angel kisses
and strong white thighs.

I have long eyelashes
and dark brown hair.

I have lines and curves
everywhere.

I shall not apologize,
for this body of mine.

It supports me.
And it continues to
Every.
Single.
Day.

LIVING FULLY

In the future,
I hope to —

Love without boundaries,
Laugh in the face of perfection,
& Constantly strive for improvement.

THE HERE AND NOW

Throughout my school years,
I spent all of my time
focusing on the future.

And now that I'm through with school,
I hope I can spend my future
focusing on the present.

SNOWFLAKES

If I could bestow a miracle
on each and every one of you
I would make sure that you knew
just how special you really are.

BE YOURSELF

Be kind.
Be gentle.
Be strong.
Be fierce.
Be independent.

Be whatever you need to be
to provide the best damn life
that you can for yourself.

REMEMBER

Success
is something to aim for,
but don't be fooled.

There's still a chance
you might wake up
successful & unhappy.

Therefore,
it's important to know
that success ≠ happiness.

Define each for yourself,
and start your journey
towards them.

You deserve to be
happy & successful,
I can promise you that.

FOREVER SEARCHING

Do not look
for happiness in love.

Instead,
find happiness
& love will come.

WANDERLUST

These days
everyone wants to wander,
but what
does wandering really entail?

If it were up to me,
I would wander around the world.

I would travel from country to country,
embracing cultures and moving freely.

I would go from place to place
without a plan and instead,
wander where the world leads me.

Wanderlust isn't just about traveling,
it's about exploring the world
and all that it has to offer.

I hope to wander
in my future.

GOD ALMIGHTY

I hope
for my future self's sake,
that God truly does
have a plan for me.

A plan that I can embrace
and lean on in my moments of doubt.

A plan that will ultimately
give my life purpose.

A plan that will inspire me
and help me inspire others.

NATURAL BLOOD THINNERS

Don't hesitate
to find family
in friendships.

Because blood
isn't always
thicker than water.

BE HEARD

There is power in silence,
but there is also power in —

Using your voice for good,
Fighting for what you believe in,
Supporting the wellbeing of others,
& Working towards building a better future.

DETERMINED

My circumstances
do not define me.

I will break every shell
and every ceiling
and every stigma
that gets in my way.

HALLELUJAH

I have high hopes,
for a future
that awaits me.

For I know,
that my God
has a plan for me.

WISHFUL THINKING

Maybe it's wishful thinking
but I hope for the day when —

I have my own personal library,
I have published my own books,
I have shared my story with the world,
& I have made a difference in someone else's life.

I hope for a life that makes me happy
and a love that brings me joy.

COINCIDENCE?

So often,
I question God.

I wonder
what His plan is for me.

Yet at times,
I can't help but think to myself,
that this is where He wants me to be.

THE FUTURE IS NEAR

Every now and then
each of us needs to be
reminded of our future.

Where we stand,
What we're working towards,
& What we're doing to get there.

This is your reminder.

PATIENCE

There will come a day,
all too quickly,
when everything
will fall into place.

The broken pieces of you,
will be restored
and your pain
will evaporate.

You will find —
Happiness
Joy
& Bliss.

You just have to be patient.

FUCK 'EM

It took a while
for me to learn
how to love myself.

But now that I have
I can honestly say
to hell with everyone else.

I AM A WOMAN

Strong
Fierce
& Resilient.

Don't forget,
that you are too.

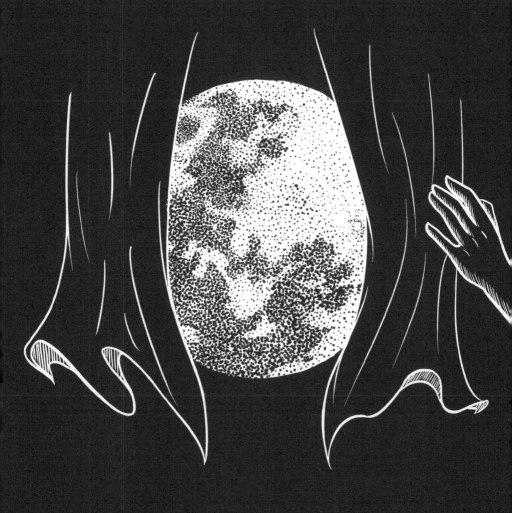

The End

FINAL MESSAGE

I hope each time you read this,
you learn something new about yourself.

I hope that you look at your pain and your past,
and you find the motivation to prevail.

I hope you see just how strong you are,
and you continuing pushing forward.

ACKNOWLEDGMENTS

First and foremost, I want to thank my great grandparents for everything they've ever done for me. No matter the circumstances, they were there for me in my most difficult and trying times, and that's all I could have ever asked for.

Up next, I want to thank Molly Brodak, Shirley A. Aaron, and all of the other writers that I've met along the way. But most importantly, I want to thank these two for encouraging me to share my story despite the fears that come with it because even if it only helped one, and upset many, it was still worth it.

To my beta readers: Stephanie, Sarah, and Alyssa; y'all have absolutely no idea how terrifying it was to put these pages in your hands. With my heart on the line, you gently gave me feedback, but more than that, you shared your stories with me. Your honesty and your responses were all I never knew I needed, and I appreciate them more than you could ever know.

And to all of the strangers, the one's that encouraged me to publish and to follow my passions, you always found me at the times that I doubted myself the most. And to the boy from Nebraska, thank you for acknowledging my fears and encouraging me anyways.

Special thanks to the incredible artists that helped me bring my vision to life. Paz Cravero you took the exact idea I had in my head and made it better than I ever expected possible. And Zed Baldemor, I don't know how you did it, but you took my words and connected them with a piece of me I hadn't even shared with you to create the most beautiful concept.

Last but least, I want to thank you. I wrote this book for myself, but I published it for you. No matter what anyone else says, you are amazing. You have made it through every good and bad day and you will continue to do so. Your story is incredible, and I appreciate you taking the time to read mine 🖤

ABOUT THE AUTHOR

Ivy Cirillo is an author, mentor, and speaker. She's a loving daughter and encouraging sister, and she's built her brand as a blogger, social media marketer, photographer, and podcaster. She loves collecting antique typewriters, concert tickets, and passport stamps and she'll never turn down a good barcade. She'll challenge you to a game of darts and encourage you to pursue your dreams in between rounds. She's forever wandering, but calls Florida home and she self-published her debut book, *Unveiled: A Poetry Memoir*, under The Orion Publishing House.

CONNECT WITH IVY CIRILLO

www.ivycirillo.com
ivycirillo@gmail.com
twitter.com/cirilloivy
facebook.com/cirilloivy
instagram.com/cirilloivy
goodreads.com/cirilloivy

Made in the USA
Middletown, DE
29 December 2019